Truth or Consequences

Biblical Truths

By
Kathleen Rutt

Copyright © 2014 by Kathleen Rutt

Truth Or Consequence
Biblical Truths
by Kathleen Rutt

Printed in the United States of America

ISBN 9781498422871

All rights reserved solely by the author. The author guarantees all contents are original and do not infringe upon the legal rights of any other person or work. No part of this book may be reproduced in any form without the permission of the author. The views expressed in this book are not necessarily those of the publisher.

Scripture quotations taken from the King James Version (KJV) – *public domain*

www.xulonpress.com

Dedication

This book is dedicated to the Lord Jesus Christ for the glory of God. His desires are in all the pages of the Weekly Bible Illustrations. His desire is for us to meditate in His word and bring forth the Fruit of the Spirit in our lives.

This book is also dedicated to all my friends, neighbors, and family.

Acknowledgments

*I*t is with great appreciation that I honor the editor of this book who is my very good friend. She corrected many errors that I made in punctuation. As led by the Holy Spirit, she also added a few scriptures. If you are in need of an editor, I can highly recommend Carla Bruce.

I want to show my appreciation to my 8 grandchildren who submitted various photo's and my daughter Faith who corrected mistakes via the computer.

Contents

Introduction 1

January UNDERSTANDING GOD 5

February UNDERSTANDING GOD'LOVE 13

March WIND OF THE SPIRIT 19

April SHOWERS OF BLESSINGS 29

May BLOSSOMS 39

June BRIDES 47

July LET FREEDOM RING 55

August SOWING SEED 63

September ENTER GOD'S REST 71

October HARVEST GROWTH 79

November THANKSFULNESS 87

December NEW BIRTH 95

Consequences 103

Introduction

The Holy Spirit directed me to write a book about the importance of His Word. I want to include all truths I have learned through these 84 years that the Lord has allowed me to live. I also want to express the consequence of not believing truth. This book is written to honor our Lord Jesus Christ and many who are in His Kingdom doing His work. His Word tells us that He will bless the work of our hands. I know His blessings are upon this book to accomplish His purposes in all who read it.

I have learned many truths by the help of ministers of God's Word, and many who are in the Body of Christ. As Christians, many of us know that Jesus Christ is the Great Physician who heals us. However, some of us have doubted that we need to go to a doctor for a check-up or for other health issues. I know that I used to think this myself, but the Lord showed me that He uses those in the health-care profession to help us. The Lord directs our footsteps and sometime He leads us to those who have the skill and education to help us. Many are in His Kingdom working for the Glory of God. I desire to honor ministers of the gospel, policemen, firemen, teachers, nurses, doctors, and many others who work in God's Kingdom for our protection, health, and growth

I especially want to honor Dr. Trim Nguyen MD, and all the nurses working with him. God has used him to care for me for the last three years. He is full of God's loving kindness and his patients are treated like people instead of numbers. The Word tells us to honor whom honor is due. I do

Introduction

---

appreciate him and he is a wonderful heart doctor. I would recommend him to anyone searching for a good heart specialist.

I have taught children for 50 years and I am well aware of many children who have fears of the unknown. As a child I always believed anything I was told. I believed anything an adult would say to me. I remember when I was in the first grade I was put in a class called "P" which meant that I was a poor learner. Little did they know that I couldn't see the blackboard because I was near sighted. Many of God's children are wounded by what adults say to them. Don't be guilty of saying to a child, "You are dumb, you will never amount to anything, I am sorry I had you, you are in my way, or other words that wound a child. Those wounds are carried throughout their lives. I know this because I have counseled many adults with problems from their childhood. Only Jesus can set them free when they forgive everyone who has wounded them.

It is so important to know that God sent His only Son to give His life for us so we can all be made into the likeness of Christ. We are God's workmanship.

As you progress through this book of weekly devotional verses, let the truth of God's Word set you free. The Word of God is Yea and Amen. It is full of Good News and it has an answer to all your questions and a solution to all your problems.

The weekly verses begin on the first day of January. This book is different from a daily devotional as the Holy Spirit desires us to understand that in repetition we will be able to daily quote His Word and it will become life to us who believe. Each page of the weekly verses has space for you to write any thoughts or ideas that come to you as you meditate on the verse.

January

Understanding God

God wants us to understand who He is and to be established in His Word. He desires us to know, that by His Grace, He gave us the Word. Jesus is His Word, as John 1:1-2 says, "In the beginning was the Word, and the Word was with God. The same was in the beginning with God." Jesus said, I am the way, the truth, and the life, no man cometh unto the Father, but by me."

January 1-7

Exodus 31:3, "God fills us with WISDOM, UNDERSTANDING, AND KNOWLEDGE; and all manner of WORKMANSHIP."

It is through confessing the Word that it becomes life to you.

On the remainder of this page, write any thoughts or ideas that come to you as you meditate on this verse.

January 8-14

Proverbs 4:7, "WISDOM is the principle thing; therefore get WISDOM; and with all getting get UNDERSTANDING."

Many Christians do not understand that God's ways are higher than our ways.

As you meditate on this verse, ask God to show you His wisdom and help you to understand His ways. Write below any thoughts you have regarding this.

January 15-21

1 John 5:20, "And we know that the Son of God is come and has given us an understanding, that we may know Him that is true, and we are in Him that is true, even in the Son Jesus Christ. This is the true God and Eternal Life."

God wants us to understand that only in His Son Jesus will we find what is true.

List below some of the truths you know about Jesus.

January 22-29

Proverbs 2:6, "For the Lord gives WISDOM; out of His mouth cometh KNOWLEDGE AND UNDERSTANDING." (Read all of Proverbs 2.)

We are told to speak the Word. When we say what God says, that Word brings wisdom, knowledge, and understanding.

Write below your thoughts about how God has given you wisdom, knowledge, and understanding.

January 30-31

1 Kings 3:9, Give, therefore, thy servant an UNDERSTANDING HEART to judge thy people, that I may discern between good and bad."

God was very pleased with King Solomon's request and gave him a wise and understanding heart. God also told him what else He would do for him if he followed His Commandments.

Write below any understanding God gives as you meditate on these verses.

FEBRUARY

UNDERSTANDING THE LOVE OF GOD

God is love and all that He does is motivated by that love. The love of God is so much greater than our human concepts of love. Only through a mind renewed by His Word can we begin to understand God's love.

February 1-7

John 3:16, "For God so loved the world, that He gave His only begotten Son, that whosoever believeth in Him should not perish, but have everlasting life."

Many people quote this verse, but many do not understand that the life of God is within them. He abides in us and will never leave us. Many Christians have doubted their salvation at various times. If we have asked Jesus to come into our hearts and save us from our sins, then He has done what He said He would do. Only believe, as all things are possible

As you meditate on this verse throughout the week, write down what it means to you.

February 8-14

1 John 4:18, "There is no fear in love; but perfect love cast out all fear because fear hath torment. He that feareth is not made perfect in love."

To be perfect in love means to mature in God's love. GOD desires us to understand how much HE LOVES US.

Write below any thoughts you have about maturing and becoming perfect in God's love.

February 15-21

1 John 4:10-11, "Herein is LOVE, not that we loved God, but that He loved us, and sent His son to be a propitiation for our sins. Beloved, if God so loved us, we ought to also love one another."

Consider how much God loves you. Are you walking in the truth of Jesus' new covenant of love?

Write below any thoughts on this subject.

February 22-29

1 Peter 3:8-9, "Finally, be ye all of one mind, having compassion one of another, love as brethren, be pitiful, be courteous; not rendering evil for evil, or railing for railing; but on the contrary, blessing, knowing that ye are called to this, that ye should inherit a blessing."

As believers, we are called by God to love one another, to be compassionate and courteous. The outcome of doing this is that we will inherit a blessing.

Write below how you could apply this truth to people whom you know.

MARCH

WIND OF THE SPIRIT

In the State of Illinois, where I grew up, we always considered March to be the month of winds. I felt led to speak and learn this month about the WIND OF THE SPIRIT. We know and we understand that we cannot see the wind. We can only see the results of the wind.

The March winds gently blow or can be very violent and cause much damage. I have seen the results of a tornado, hurricane, and many violent windstorms. I prefer feeling a gentle wind blowing through the trees and upon my face. The Holy Spirit cannot be seen either. When Jesus arose from the dead, He sent His Holy Spirit to all of those who would accept Him as their Savior. In Mathew 3:11-12, John the Baptist said, "I indeed baptize you with water unto repentance: but He that cometh after me is mightier than I, whose shoes I am not worthy to bear: He shall baptize you with the Holy Ghost, and with fire, whose fan is in His hand, and he will thoroughly purge His floor, and gather His wheat into the garner; but he will burn up the chaff with unquenchable fire."

The Holy Ghost was poured out in Acts 2 when they were in one accord. Acts 2:17, 18, "And it shall come to pass in the last days, saith God, I will pour out of my Spirit upon all flesh; and your sons and your daughters shall prophesy, and your young men shall see visions, and your old men shall dream dreams. And on my servants and on my handmaidens, I will pour out in those days of my Spirit and they shall prophesy."

The Holy Ghost is our teacher, comforter, helper, and power. In our day there are many who do not understand that the infilling of the Holy Ghost will allow us to speak in other tongues. God has used speaking in tongues to build up my faith. He allowed me to minister to a lady from Romania who could not communicate with anyone. She kissed me on both cheeks as I kept praying in tongues. She did not want to let go of me and waved kisses at me when I left. The next week an interpreter came and she was able to communicate. God uses me in intercessory prayer for others in this same way. Speaking in tongues is also "Praising the Lord."

March 1-7

Ephesians 6:10, "Be strong in the Lord and in the power of His might."

To be strong in the Lord and walk in His power means that we understand who He is and what He can do.

As you meditate on this verse, list any areas where you are strong in the Lord, as well as areas in which you need help.

March 8-14

1 John 4:12-13, "No man hath seen God at anytime. If we love one another God dwelleth in us, and His love is perfected in us. By this know we that we dwell in Him, and He is in us, because He hath given us of His Spirit."

God has given us His Holy Spirit so that we might know that God dwells in us and we dwell in Him. God doesn't want us to doubt that He dwells in us; He wants us to KNOW.

As you meditate on this scripture, write your thoughts below.

March 15-21

Psalm 46:1, "God is our refuge and strength, a very present help in the time of trouble."

We all have times of trouble. How encouraging to know that God is our very present help.

Write below what this verse means to you and how you have experienced its reality.

March 22-28

Psalm 9:9-10, "The Lord also will be a refuge for the oppressed, a refuge in times of trouble. And they who know thy name will put their trust in thee; for thou, Lord, hast not forsaken those who seek thee."

When we seek the Lord, we can be assured that He will not forsake us. We can trust Him.

Write below any areas in which you are seeking the Lord.

March 29-31

John 4:7-8, "Beloved, let us love one another; for love is of God; and everyone that loveth is born of God, and knoweth God. He that loveth not knoweth not God, for GOD IS LOVE

We CAN love one another because we are born of God.

Write below your thoughts and insight into these verses.

April

Showers of Blessings

I doubt if anyone can count all the blessings that God has bestowed upon them. I know that all these years He has blessed me abundantly and given me my heart's desires.

I have had many trials and tests to prove that I trust God with all my heart, soul, and mind.

On November 15, 1985, I was in an accident and immediately with the Lord. I was thrown out of a truck and my grandson Jason was also thrown out. We were both instantly in heaven together. My husband was over my body calling life back to me. The Lord told me as Lazarus was called forth from the tomb, that I was called forth from the grave. My husband told Jason to call out to Jesus. Jason was almost four years old and obeyed and called out to Jesus. At the hospital, the doctors said that Jason would never fully recover because of the injury to his brain.

As they were ready to put a bolt in his brain, he awoke. The Spirit of the Lord hovered over him and healed him. He has a very good testimony of what the Lord Jesus did for him in heaven. God gave him a miracle. I was in intensive care for ten days. God gave me a divine healing.

I could not get better until I saw Jason was healed. When I saw him in my hospital room, I said to him, "Jason, because of you, Grandma is going to get better." On the tenth day, I was taken out of intensive care. I was in the hospital 40 days and 40 nights. No matter what I have gone thru these 84 years of my life, God has always been faithful to me and delivered me. My healing came through reading the Word of God and all the prayers of the Body of Christ. Psalm 34:19, "Many are the afflictions of the righteous; but the Lord delivers him from them all."

I am not righteous, but Jesus Christ in me has made me righteous.

April 1-4

Psalm 103:3, "He forgiveth all our iniquities; and healeth all our diseases."

Think about it! ALL...ALL...ALL. Nothing is too hard for him.

As you think about this verse, write below how this truth has come to pass in your life. Or how you would like for it to.

April 5-11

Isaiah 57:19, "I create the fruit of the lips; Peace, peace to him that is afar off, and to him that is near; saith the Lord; and I will heal him."

It's easy to feel at peace when we think the Lord is near. But God promises peace to us even if we afar off. Peace from God doesn't depend on where we are, but WHO GOD IS.

Write below some of the times God has given you peace.

April 12-18

Isaiah 40:29, "He giveth power to the faint; and to them that have no might He increaseth strength."

What a promise! He gives power and strength to us when we need it.

As you meditate on this verse, write down how it has been applied in your life, or how you would like God to apply it right now.

April 19-25

Galatians 3:13-14, "Christ hath redeemed us from the curse of the law, being made a curse for us; for it is written, Cursed is everyone that hangeth on a tree; that the Blessings of Abraham might come on the Gentiles through Jesus Christ; that we might receive the promise of the Spirit through faith."

Redeemed is such a powerful concept. And God has redeemed us through the sacrifice of Jesus Christ.

Write below what it means to you to be redeemed from the curse of the law.

April 26-30

1 John 5:20, "And we know that the Son of God is come, and hath given us an understanding, that we may know Him that is true, and we are in Him that is true, even in His Son Jesus Christ, This is the true God, and eternal life."

We know Him, and we are in Him. This is eternal life.

Write below what this truth means to you.

May

Blossoms

During the month of May, we are overjoyed at the beauty of all the different flowers in bloom. They are perfect in design by the great God of the Universe. In heaven, flowers are like velvet. One cannot explain the beauty that God has waiting for all who have accepted Jesus Christ as their Savior.

As flowers begin to blossom on earth so do many born again Christians. When we are young in the Lord, we start learning what it is to drink the milk of the Word. As we eat and drink daily bread and milk, it is very important to drink and eat spiritual food. As we grow, we begin to eat the meat of God's word by meditating in His Word. I have learned so much by the good things God has given unto us to enjoy. By meditating in His word, our spiritual understanding begins to grow.

May 1-2

Song of Solomon 2:1, "I [Jesus] am the Rose of Sharon and the Lily of the Valley."

Mathew 6:28-29, "And why take ye thought for raiment? Consider the lilies of the field, how they grow; they toil not, neither do they spin. And yet I say unto you, even Solomon in all his glory was not arrayed like one of these."

Many lessons can be learned from thinking about the beauty of God's creation—especially the flowers. It's no accident that a rose and a lily are used to describe Jesus.

Look at the flowers around you with enlightened eyes, and ask God to reveal the meaning of their beauty. Write below any thoughts that come to you while meditating on these verses.

May 3-9

Galatians 6:7, "Be not deceived; God is not mocked: for whatsoever a man soweth, that shall he also reap."

Just as a farmer chooses what seeds to sow in his fields, so we always have a choice of what seeds we will sow in our lives and in the lives of others. Ask God to help you sow good seeds, and if you have sown bad seeds, ask His forgiveness.

As you meditate on this verse throughout the week, list below the good seeds you have sown.

May 10-16

Galatians 6:9, "And let us not be weary in well doing: for in due season we shall reap, if we faint not."

Since God's seasons are not the same as ours, the "due season" for reaping the harvest of the seeds we have sown is in God's hands.

This week think about the some of the blessings you have reaped in the past and list them here.

May 17-23

Ephesians 1:13, "In whom ye also trusted, after that ye heard the word of truth, the gospel of your salvation: in whom also after that ye believed, ye were sealed with that Holy Spirit of promise."

This verse reminds us of the One (Jesus) in whom we have trusted and that we are "sealed" with Holy Spirit. When something is sealed, it's official—it's a done deal.

Write below what it means to you to be sealed with the Holy Spirit of promise.

May 24-30

Ephesians 5:18, "And be not drunk with wine, wherein is excess; but be filled with the Spirit.

God revealed many revelations when I was baptized in the Holy Spirit. He has answered so many prayers. That is why I am so thankful for the blessing of the gift of speaking in tongues, which builds up our faith and teaches us to pray the perfect prayer of the Father for others. 1 Corinthians 14:2 declares, "He who speaketh in an unknown tongue speaketh not unto men, but unto God: for no man understandeth him, howbeit in the Spirit he speaketh mysteries." Jesus is the same yesterday today and forever. All of His gifts are available to those who will believe.

This week, consider what it means to be filled with the Spirit and write your thoughts below.

June

Brides

All believers are the Bride of Christ. He is coming for a Bride without spot or wrinkle. The Word of God tells us that we have a new name in glory. We will all sit at the banqueting table that is prepared for us. We will be living in a new and better place.

The Lord is preparing all of us to be the Bride of Christ. Think of the many things a bride does before she marries the man of her dreams. A bride is filled with excitement knowing soon she will be given a new name. She must get her gown in perfect order without any spots or wrinkles. She makes plans for where the wedding will be. She makes a list of the guests. She chooses what food will be served at the reception ad selects a beautiful wedding cake. She also knows that she will be going to a new home and meeting new people.

June 1-6

Isaiah 61:10, "I will greatly rejoice in the Lord, my soul shall be joyful in my God, for He hath clothed me with the Garments of Salvation, He hath covered me with the Robe of Righteousness, as a Bridegroom decketh himself with ornaments, and as a Bride adorneth herself with her jewels.

We have great reason to rejoice when we consider that God has clothed us with garments of Salvation and robes of Righteousness.

As you think about this truth, picture yourself clothed in salvation and righteousness and write any thoughts you have about this below.

June 7-13

Isaiah 62:5b, "As the Bridegroom rejoiceth over the Bride, so shall thy God rejoice over thee."

Just as there is great rejoicing at a wedding, so God the Father rejoices over His Son's Bride.

Write below what it means to you to be the Bride of Christ.

June 14-20

Jeremiah 33:11, "The voice of joy, and the voice of gladness, the voice of the Bridegroom, and the voice of the Bride, the voice of them that shall say, Praise the Lord of hosts; for the Lord is good; for His mercy endureth forever...."

The theme of joy and rejoicing continues with this verse. We can rejoice because God's mercy endures forever.

As you meditate on this verse, write your thoughts below.

June 21-27

John 3:28-29, "Ye yourselves bear me witness, that I said I am not the Christ, but that I am sent before Him He that hath the Bride is the Bridegroom: but the friend of the Bridegroom, which standeth and heareth Him, rejoiceth greatly because of the Bridegroom's voice; this my joy therefore, is fulfilled."

John the Baptist identified himself as the friend of the Bridegroom who stood with him and heard him. This caused John's joy to be fulfilled.

As you meditate on this verse, think about times when your joy was fulfilled and write them below.

June 28-30

Revelation 22:17, "And the Spirit and the Bride say, Come. And let him that heareth say, Come. And let him that is athirst come. And whosoever will, let him take the water of life freely."

We all are excited to attend a wedding. Can you imagine how excited we will be when Jesus comes for His Bride.

We who are His Bride must be ready when our Bridegroom comes to take us to our heavenly home. In the parable of the ten virgins (Matthew 25:1-13), verse 13 says, "Watch therefore, for ye know neither the day nor the hour wherein the Son of man cometh."

As you meditate on these verses, write your thoughts below.

July

Let Freedom Ring

Thank God that we live in a country where we are free to worship our Lord and Savior Jesus Christ. Many countries are in bondage to their leaders. Not only does God desire for us to be free, but He has provided the way to freedom in Jesus. "If the Son therefore shall make you FREE ye shall be FREE indeed." John 8:36.

July 1-4

Isaiah 58:6, "Is not this the fast that I have chosen? To loose the bands of wickedness, to undo the heavy burdens, and to let the oppressed go FREE, and that you break every yoke?"

This verse links fasting as a path to breaking the hold of wickedness and undoing heavy burdens. While God has given us other paths to freedom, we should not neglect fasting when we sense the Lord leading us to do so.

Write below any thoughts you have about this verse and about fasting.

July 5-11

John 8:32, "And ye shall know the TRUTH, and the TRUTH shall make you FREE."

All of God's Word is TRUTH. We may not understand all of it, but as we read and study the Word, we will come to understand more and more. To know truth is a lifetime journey.

Have you experienced the freedom that comes from knowing truth? Mention it below.

July 12-18

Romans 6:18, "Being then made FREE from sin, ye became the servants of righteousness."

When we receive Jesus as our Savior, He not only frees us from sin but also makes it possible for us to be servants of righteousness. What a glorious position we have in Christ!

Write below what it means to you to be free from sin and a servant of righteousness.

July 19-25

Romans 8:2, "For the law of the Spirit in Christ Jesus hath made me FREE from the law of sin and death."

There are many kinds of laws—some are man-made and subject to change; others, like the laws of nature, are inherent or built-in. Then there are spiritual laws that cannot be changed. These are the highest laws and they are greater than any other. As the verse above says, "The law of the Spirit in Jesus makes us free from the law of sin and death." That's a powerful law.

Write below the ways you see this truth applied in your life.

July 26-31

Galatians 5:1, "Stand fast therefore in the LIBERTY wherewith Christ hath made us FREE, and be not entangled again with the yoke of bondage."

Men and women gave their lives to establish the United States of America, and throughout the years since then, hundreds of thousands have given their lives to protect and preserve that freedom. Christ gave His life that we might have a freedom even greater than that. This verse reminds us to stand fast in that liberty and not allow ourselves to go into bondage of any kind.

Write below any thoughts you have about your liberty in Christ.

August

Sowing Seed

We all want to sow good seed to everyone we meet along this journey that we are taking to the Promised Land. An important part of sowing good seed is directly related to what we allow into our minds. If we allow thoughts of doubt and unbelief into our minds, then it is difficult for faith to arise within us. The Word of God renews our minds and fills us with good seed to sow in our lives and in the lives of others.

August 1

Philippians 4:19, "But my God shall supply all your need according to His riches in glory by Christ Jesus."

Do you really believe this? Do you live like you believe this verse, or do you worry and fret about obtaining what you need?

As you focus on this verse, write down specific areas where you need to believe that God will meet your needs.

August 2-8,

Mark 4:14, "The Sower soweth the Word."

It is so important to know the Word of God and to sow the relevant seeds of His Word into our lives. For example, if you are sick in your body, read Psalm 103:3. Sow those words into your heart. God has given us the Bible, and it is filled with promises that will bring forth a harvest of blessing in our lives.

As you meditate on this verse, sow some good seeds into your life. List them here.

August 9-15

Psalm 126:5, "They that sow in tears shall reap in joy."

When we are in the midst of troubling and sorrowful times, it is so important to sow the seeds of faith that will eventually bring us joy.

List below the times you have sown in tears.

August 16-22

2 Corinthians 9:10, "Now He that ministereth seed to the sower both minister bread for your food, and multiply your seed sown, and increase the fruits of your righteousness."

This verse is part of a prayer the Apostle Paul prayed for believers in Corinth. He understood the importance of sowing the good seed of the Gospel of Jesus Christ.

Meditate on this verse and write below how it can apply to you.

August 23-29

Proverbs 11:30, "The fruit of the righteous is a tree of life; and he that winneth souls is wise."

Good seeds lead to righteous fruit and this verse says that is a "tree of life." Also, when we sow the Word of salvation into those around us, we are wise.

Write below how this verse applies to you.

August 30-31

Galatians 6:9-10, "And let us not be weary in well doing: for in due season we shall reap, if we faint not. As we have, therefore, opportunity, let us do good unto all men, especially unto them who are of the household of faith."

God understands that when we have to wait a long time to see results from the good seed we sow, it's easy to get discouraged and give up. This verse encourages us to not be weary in doing good, for we will reap the good harvest of our actions in due season—in God's time.

Write below any people or circumstances that you have given up on. And then sow some more good seed.

SEPTEMBER

ENTER GOD'S REST

Rest is essential to our well-being. We rest when we are tired, sick, and stressed out. Doctors understand the importance of rest and will often prescribe "bed rest" along with needed medication. But God has a spiritual rest that goes beyond rest in the natural. We enter God's rest when we trust Him completely to guide us, to provide for us, and to walk in the "works He has prepared for us—the works that bring glory to His name.

September 1-5

Isaiah 28:11, "For with stammering lips and another tongue will He speak to this people. To whom He said, This is the Rest wherewith ye may cause the weary to Rest: and this is the refreshing: Yet they would not believe."

There is a type of rest associated with the gift of speaking in other tongues. We may not understand exactly how this works, but when we participate in this gift, we reap its built-in benefits.

As you meditate on this verse, write your thoughts below.

September 6-12

Jeremiah 6:16, "Thus saith the Lord, Stand ye in the ways, and see and ask for the old paths, where is the good way, and walk therein, and ye shall find Rest for your souls. But they said, We will not walk therein."

God's ways are eternal. They do not change from one generation to another or from century to century. When people adopt ways of living that are contrary to God's ways, there is no true rest.

Can you relate to this verse? Write below how it speaks to you.

September 13-19

Mathew 11:28-29 "Come unto me, all ye that labour and are heavy laden, and I will give you Rest. Take My Yoke upon you, and Learn of Me; for I am meek and lowly in heart: and ye shall find Rest unto your souls."

When we are yoked with Jesus and learn of Him, we walk in step with Him. We have rest in our souls as we move forward.

List below any areas in which you need God's rest.

September 20-26

Hebrews 3:18, "And to whom sware He that they should not enter into His Rest, but to them that believed not."

This verse refers to the Children of Israel when they were wandering in the wilderness after God delivered them from bondage in Egypt.

Do you have wilderness areas in your life where you need to believe that God can and will deliver you? Write them here.

September 27-30

Hebrews 4:9, "There remaineth therefore a Rest to the people of God."

Even though we struggle at times in our own strength and abilities to accomplish something, God remains faithful and waits for us to believe His Word and enter into His rest. That rest remains.

Write below what this verse means to you

October

Harvest Growth

During the month of October it is so refreshing to see all of the beautiful leaves upon the trees. When we lived in Elgin, Illinois I loved going up and down the roads beholding the trees in all their splendid colors. We had a pathway full of colorful trees.

October 1-3

Mark 4:29, "But when the fruit is brought forth, immediately He putteth in the sickle, because the Harvest is come."

Just as harvest times vary in the natural according to the kind of fruit or vegetable, so harvest times in the Kingdom of God also vary from person to person. God alone knows when to reap the harvest of His Word in our lives.

As you consider this truth, write your thoughts below.

October 4-10

Mathew 9:37, "Then saith He to His disciples, The Harvest truly is plenteous, but the labourers are few."

God needs workers to harvest His fields. As believers we are those workers. We need to stay tuned in to Him so that if He says, "Go here" or "Go there," we are prepared.

Write below your thoughts about this verse.

October 11-17

Luke 10:2, "The harvest truly is great, but the labourers are few: pray ye therefore the Lord of the Harvest, that He would send forth labourers into His Harvest."

The Lord spoke these words to the 70 disciples that He sent forth into every city and place where He planned to go. While this verse is similar to the one from last week, God adds to it by saying that we are to pray to the Lord of the Harvest that He would send workers into His Harvest. So prayer is a necessary part of bringing in the Harvest.

Think about this verse and write any thoughts below.

October 18-24

John 4:35, "Say not ye, There are yet four months, and then cometh Harvest? behold, I say unto you, Lift up your eyes, and look on the fields; for they are white already to Harvest."

This verse deals with the timing of the harvest—when it is ripe for picking. It seems that in the natural, we may think that time remains before the harvest, but when we view things as God does, we see that the fields are ready to harvest. We need God's perspective.

How does this verse apply to you? Write your thoughts below.

October 25-31

Mathew 13:30 "Let both grow together until the Harvest; and in the time of Harvest: I will say to the reapers, Gather ye together first the tares, and bind them in bundles to burn them: but gather the Wheat into My Barn."

See Matthew 13:24-30, which is the Parable of the Wheat and the Tares. The tares are weeds that the enemy sows in the field where good seed has been sown. While our first thought might be to pull up the tares as soon as they appear, God knows better. He will deal with the tares, but in His time.

Write below how this truth speaks to you.

November

Thankfulness

November is the time in which we are to give God our thankfulness for all He has given us to enjoy. I really like Thanksgiving time when families can gather together to glorify our Father in Heaven. I always enjoyed having friends and loved ones enjoy Thanksgiving Day with our family in Camp Verde, Arizona. What a wonderful time we had!

November 1-7

Psalm 136:26, "Oh, give Thanks to the God of Heaven; for His Mercy endureth forever."

There are many reasons to give thanks to God, but for this week we want to focus on giving thanks for God's everlasting mercy. We all need His mercy.

Write below some of the thoughts you have about God's enduring mercy and how you have experienced it.

November 8-14

Psalm 100:4, "Enter into His gates with Thanksgiving, and into His courts with Praise: be thankful unto Him, and Bless His name."

This verse invites us to come into His presence with thanksgiving and praise. We can do this in our times of private prayer and when we come together with other believers.

As you put this verse into practice this week, write your thoughts below.

Thankfulness

November 15-21

Philippians 4:6, "Be anxious for nothing; but in everything by prayer and supplication with Thanksgiving let your requests be made known unto God."

When we go to God in thankfulness and prayer with our requests, anxiety and worry will be far from our thoughts.

Put this verse into practice this week, and write the results below.

November 22-28

1 Thessalonians 5:18, "In everything give Thanks: for this is the Will of God in Christ Jesus concerning you."

This verse can revolutionize your walk with God. Giving thanks in everything puts our focus on God, not the situation or problem. Even in the most difficult circumstances, we know that God is with us—and for that we give thanks.

Write below how you have practiced this truth this week.

Thankfulness

November 29-30

Psalm 92:1, "It is a good thing to give thanks unto the Lord, and to sing praises unto thy name, O Most High."

Giving thanks is always a good thing. Our spirits are lifted when we sing praises to our God. Our thoughts always turn from negative to positive when we give thanks.

As you practice giving thanks this week, write below how it affects you.

December

New Birth

In December, our thoughts turn to preparations for the Christmas season. Christians delight in celebrating and remembering the Birth of our Lord and Savior Jesus Christ. The world is trying to take Christ out of Christmas. They are replacing it with, "Happy Holidays." I will always say, Merry Christmas no matter what the world says. This is a time of giving and enjoying family, friends, and sharing with those in need. "Merry Christmas to all."

December 1-5

Isaiah 43:19, Behold, I will do a NEW THING; now it shall spring forth; shall ye not know it? I will even make a way in the wilderness, and rivers in the desert."

This is a promise that we can claim and experience throughout our lives. God will do a new thing and make a way for us when we are in a "wilderness" of hurt, disappointment, or trials.

Write below what this promise means to you.

December 6-12

John 13:34-35, "A NEW COMMANDMENT I give unto you, that ye love one another; as I have loved you, that ye also love one another. By this shall all men know that ye are my disciples, if ye have love one to another."

This "new commandment" of loving one another could change the world—one person at a time.

Is this an easy or a difficult commandment for you? Write your thoughts below.

December 13-19

John 3:6-7, "That which is born of the flesh is flesh; and that which is born of the Spirit is spirit. Marvel not that I said unto thee, ye must be BORN AGAIN."

Jesus was speaking with Nicodemus, a ruler of the Jews, who didn't understand how a man could be born again. In John 3:16, Jesus said that when we believe in Him we will not perish but have everlasting life. This is the NEW BIRTH. This is Salvation.

Have you experienced the new birth in Christ?

December 20-26

2 Corinthians 5:17, "Therefore if any man be in Christ, he is a new creature: old things are passed away: behold, all things are become new."

The more you think about this promise of being a new creature in Christ, the more you realize all that God has done for you.

Write below what this promise means to you.

December 27-31

Ephesians 4:24, "And that you put on the New Man, which after God is created in righteousness, and true holiness."

The "new man" is the born again man as distinguished from the old man who is dead in sins. The new man is a partaker of the divine nature and life of Christ.

Write below what this truth means to you.

Consequences

I HAVE WRITTEN TRUTH AND NOW IF YOU DO NOT BELIEVE TRUTH, THEN YOU WILL HAVE CONSEQUENCES, WHICH ARE THE FOLLOWING VERSES IN THE WORD OF GOD.

Luke 16:19-31 (PARABLE of the rich man and LAZARUS)

"There was a certain rich man, which was clothed in purple and fine linen, and fared sumptuously every day. And there was a beggar named Lazarus, which was laid at his gate, full of sores, and desiring to be fed with the crumbs from the rich man's table; moreover, the dogs came and licked his sores. Jesus began telling how the beggar was taken to the bosom of Abraham, and the rich man was in HELL and he lifted his eyes being in torments, he looked afar off and saw Lazarus in the bosom of Abraham. He cried out and said, 'Father Abraham, have mercy on me and send Lazarus, that he may dip his finger in water, and cool my tongue; for I AM TORMENTED IN THIS FLAME.' "

He wanted for his five brothers to be told about HELL, and Jesus told him about the gulf between them and if they didn't listen to Moses and the prophets that they wouldn't believe if anyone arose from the dead. (Read this whole parable and you will see that HELL is real for those who do not accept the sacrifice of our God who sent Jesus to be our Savior.

Matthew 7:21

"Not everyone that saith unto me, Lord, Lord, shall enter into the kingdom of heaven; but he that doeth the will of my Father which is in heaven."

Proverbs 15:10

"Correction is grevious unto him that hath forsaken the way: and he that hateth reproof shall die."

Matthew 7:22-23

"Many will say to me in that day, Lord, Lord, have we not prophesied in thy name? And in thy name have cast out devils? And in thy name done wonderful works? And then will I profess unto them, I never knew you: depart from me, ye that work iniquity."

Many profess to be Christians but do not really know Jesus. Many want recognition, popularity, and they follow the world instead of the narrow road to heaven. Yes, the Lord forgives all our sins and allows His Holy Spirit to make abode within us. He will bring us into victory and help us to be an overcomer. We cannot do this on our own. Without the Lord Jesus Christ, we can do nothing.

Proverbs 6:16-19

"These six things doth the Lord hate; yea, seven are an abomination unto him; a proud look, a lying tongue, and hands that shed innocent blood, an heart that deviseth wicked imaginations, feet that are swift in running to mischief, a false witness that speaketh lies, and he that soweth discord among brethren."

All of us have been guilty and that is why I am so thankful that the Lord Jesus Christ who has forgiven me of past sins and future as long as I ask forgiveness.

1 John 1:9

"If we confess our sins, He is Faithful and Just to forgive us our sins, and to cleanse us from all Unrighteousness."

My prayer is for you to come to know Jesus and understand how much He loves you. Realize that there is a Heaven and a Hell. God does not want anyone to go to Hell. He gives you the choice to take the narrow way to Heaven or the wide road to destruction. He wishes all men to be saved. That is why He sacrificed His only Son for you and me.

If you want to accept Jesus as your Saviour, please say this prayer: Lord Jesus, I come to you to ask you to forgive me of all my sins and cleanse me from all unrighteousness. I accept you as my Saviour and Lord. Thank you, Lord, for your forgiveness. Amen.

www.ingramcontent.com/pod-product-compliance
Lightning Source LLC
LaVergne TN
LVHW022000060526
838201LV00048B/1633